Belonging to :

FAMILY
Coloring Funny

FAMILY

Coloring Funny

FAMILY
Coloring Funny

FAMILY
Coloring Funny

FAMILY

Coloring Funny

FAMILY
Coloring Funny

FAMILY
Coloring Funny

FAMILY
Coloring Funny

FAMILY

Coloring Funny

FAMILY
Coloring Funny

FAMILY
Coloring Funny

FAMILY
Coloring Funny

FAMILY
Coloring Funny

FAMILY
Coloring Funny

FAMILY

Coloring Funny

FAMILY
Coloring Funny

FAMILY
Coloring Funny

FAMILY
Coloring Funny

FAMILY
Coloring Funny

FAMILY
Coloring Funny

FAMILY
Coloring Funny

FAMILY
Coloring Funny

FAMILY
Coloring Funny

FAMILY

Coloring Funny

FAMILY
Coloring Funny

FAMILY
Coloring Funny

FAMILY
Coloring Funny

FAMILY
Coloring Funny

FAMILY
Coloring Funny

FAMILY

Coloring Funny

FAMILY
Coloring Funny

FAMILY
Coloring Funny

FAMILY

Coloring Funny

FAMILY
Coloring Funny

FAMILY
Coloring Funny

FAMILY
Coloring Funny

FAMILY

Coloring Funny

FAMILY
Coloring Funny

FAMILY
Coloring Funny

FAMILY
Coloring Funny

FAMILY
Coloring Funny

FAMILY
Coloring Funny

FAMILY
Coloring Funny

FAMILY
Coloring Funny

FAMILY
Coloring Funny

FAMILY

Coloring Funny

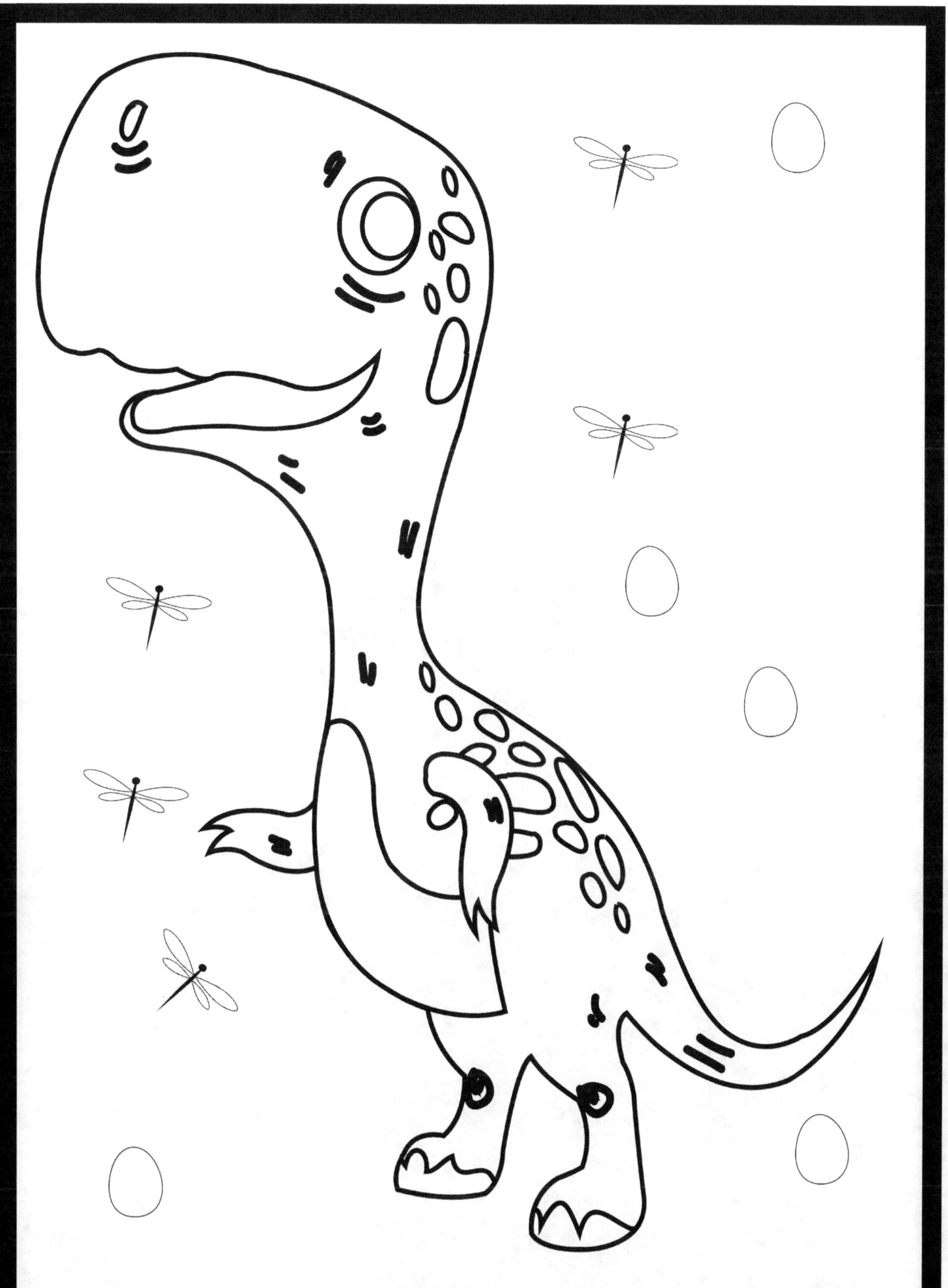

FAMILY
Coloring Funny

FAMILY
Coloring Funny

FAMILY
Coloring Funny

FAMILY
Coloring Funny

FAMILY
Coloring Funny

www.ingramcontent.com/pod-product-compliance
Lightning Source LLC
Chambersburg PA
CBHW081728250726
48657CB00010B/3178
9798580665504